WILLIAM BLAKE
Visionary Anarchist

FREEDOM PRESS publish *Freedom* (fortnightly) and *The Raven* (quarterly) as well as books (more than fifty titles in print).

FREEDOM PRESS BOOKSHOP carries the most comprehensive stock of anarchist literature including titles from North America. Please send for our current list.

> Freedom Press
> in Angel Alley
> 84b Whitechapel High Street
> London E1 7QX

DEDICATION

*For Dylan and Emily
and other poets, artists and lovers of freedom*

By the Same Author

Journey through Tanzania (Bodley Head, 1984)

William Godwin (Yale University Press, 1984)

The Anarchist Writings of William Godwin (Freedom Press, 1986)

Into Cuba (Zena, 1985, 1990)

Cuba Libre: Breaking the Chains?
 (Victor Gollancz, 1987; Unwin, 1988)

Journey through Maldives (Camerapix, 1992)

Demanding the Impossible: A History of Anarchism
 (HarperCollins, 1992; Fontana Press, 1993)

Nature's Web: An Exploration of Ecological Thinking
 (Simon & Schuster, 1992)

Around Africa: From the Pillars of Hercules to the Strait of Gibraltar
 (Simon & Schuster, 1994)

William Blake by Thomas Phillips (1807)
(By permission of the National Portrait Gallery, London)

WILLIAM BLAKE:
Visionary Anarchist

by

Peter Marshall

Freedom Press
1994

First Edition 1988

Published by
FREEDOM PRESS

84b Whitechapel High Street
London E1 7QX

Second Edition 1994

©Peter Marshall 1988, 1994
& Freedom Press

ISBN 0 900384 77 8

Printed and typeset in Great Britain by Aldgate Press
London E1 7RQ

CONTENTS

Preface	*9*
Introduction	*11*
Life	*12*
Tradition	*18*
Philosophy	*19*
Nature	*22*
Human Nature	*24*
Politics	*33*
The State	*36*
The Church	*40*
Mind-Forged Manacles	*42*
Existing Society	*47*
Free Society	*51*
Notes	*63*

ILLUSTRATIONS

'The Dance of Albion' or 'Glad Day'	*Cover illustration*
William Blake by Thomas Phillips (1807)	*Frontispiece*
Newton, measuring the Ratio (1795)	*27*
Bromion & Oothoon chained at the mouth of a cave, frontispiece of *Visions of the Daughters of Albion* (1793)	*31*
'The Ancient of Days' frontispiece of *Europe* (1794)	*43*
'Aged Ignorance', *For Children: The Gates of Paradise* (1793)	*47*
Nebuchadnezzar, symbol of reason, authority and oppression, being banished from Jerusalem	*59*
'Europe supported by Africa & America' Engraving for J. G. Stedman, *Narrative* (1796)	*61*

Preface

We are no longer living in the blissful dawn which William Blake, William Godwin and their fellow radicals experienced at the outbreak of the French Revolution two centuries ago. The triumphant State has come to intrude itself into all aspects of society, into the innermost recesses of everyday life. The oppressor still sits on the throne, in the government cabinet, on the judge's bench, at the head of the dinner table. Nevertheless, as the second millennium approaches, an increasing number of people are turning to a libertarian alternative which offers a direct form of democracy and enables individuals to govern themselves and to create their own history.

William Blake speaks directly to this growing libertarian movement. For all his misty rhetoric and craggy eloquence, his message is both simple and straightforward. Once the key to his mythology has been discovered, he is nothing like as difficult as his reputation might suggest. In swelling poetry and incisive prose, he demands bread for all and a fair return for a fair day's work. He would like to see an end to capital, tax and empire. He calls for complete sexual and racial equality and celebrates universal toleration. He rejects all forms of repression and urges the total fulfilment of sexuality. Above all, in a world where State, Church and Academy are no longer necessary, he looks forward to a time when all would be free to cultivate their mind and imagination, and to become king, priest and artist in their own home.

Blake may have been a visionary, but he was very much part of this world. He worked as an engraver when the Industrial

Revolution was threatening his craft. He longed for peace at a time of expanding war. He was born in Broad Street, off Golden Square, but he experienced the darkness of depression and felt entirely out of tune with his contemporaries. With deceit and hypocrisy abroad in the streets of London, he searched vainly for truth. But he never lost his confidence in the perfectibility of humanity and the possibility of creating a free and equal society in harmony with nature. In the fiery forge of his imagination, he shaped wondrous visions of freedom and love.

It is hoped that the present introduction to Blake's world will show something of the light which shines beyond the cloudy mountain range of his symbolism. I am indebted to Peter Cadogan for reading the text and making some useful suggestions. The British Library, the British Museum, the Tate Gallery and the National Portrait Gallery have kindly given me permission to use the illustrations. I would finally like to thank the Freedom Press Group for their friendly and caring assistance in producing this work.

Croesor, 24 May 1988

Introduction

"Madman" I have been call'd: "Fool" they call me,
I wonder which they Envy, Thee or Me?

William Blake has been nearly all things to all people. Neglected in his own lifetime, he became harnessed after his death to a whole range of disparate movements. We have had Blake the madman, the eccentric, the mystic, the prophet, the proto-Marxist and the humanist. He has been the noble savage of the over-refined and the psychedelic guru of the Flower Power generation. Some see him as a philosophical idealist, others as a historical materialist. As for his critics, they have broadly fallen into two hostile camps: those who are primarily interested in his perennial philosophy, admiring his religious and psychological insights, and those who stress his social roots and political commitment. There is still little agreement on the exact nature of his achievement.

The social and the spiritual aspects of Blake are not however exclusive. While he may have seen angels in the trees as a boy and listened to the voices of 'Messengers from Heaven', he had his feet firmly on the ground. It just happened that he considered the ground to be organized spirit rather than dead matter. Indeed, Blake's appeal lies precisely in the fact that he combined the social and the spiritual, and what we would today call the ecological. He was a revolutionary anarchist, looking back to the gnostic heresies of the Middle Ages and anticipating modern anarchism and social ecology. With William Godwin, he stands as a great forerunner of British anarchism.[1]

Although Blake's vision grew deeper and more elaborate as he grew older, there is a continuity in his social and spiritual interests. He did not abandon his early radicalism after the failure of the French Revolution and retreat into the craggy and misty wilderness of his prophetic writings.[2] Throughout his life he searched for spiritual and social freedom, and rebelled against all authority, whether in the form of State and King, Church and God, Master and Mammon. He may have thrown off the *bonnet rouge* which he sported at the time of the French Revolution when things turned bloody, but he held firm to his vision of a free society which had been first inspired by the American struggle for independence. To his last days, he remained a 'Liberty Boy'. As the poet Swinburne observed: 'To serve art and to love liberty seemed to him the two things (if indeed they were not one thing) worth a man's life and work.'[3]

Life

William Blake was born on 28 November 1757, the third of four children. He lived in an age of revolution when Britain was undergoing fundamental changes in its industrial, political and cultural life. He was born at the beginning of the Seven Years War and during most of his adulthood Britain was at war with France. But he was lucky enough to grow up in a comparatively peaceful London. His father was a hosier, neither rich nor poor, and his tolerant family lived, appropriately enough, in Broad Street off Golden Square. As a boy Blake roamed the green and pleasant fields surrounding the metropolis and swum in the river Thames. From about eight years old, he began having 'visions' and saw angels among haymakers at dawn and in a tree at Dulwich. His early experience not only meant that he knew about work and poverty at first hand but it also provided a very real basis to his later visions of innocence and freedom.

At the age of ten, he left school and entered drawing school.

Four years later he became an apprentice engraver with James Basire and learned the craft until he was twenty. When he was twenty-two, he became a student at the Royal Academy for a few months where he developed a strong dislike of its President Sir Joshua Reynolds and his concept of High Art. He particularly rejected Reynolds' advocacy of patronage and 'royal liberality': in the margin of Reynolds' *Discourse*, Blake later wrote: 'Liberality! we want not Liberality. We want a Fair Price & Proportionate Value & a General Demand for Art' (446).[4] Blake left the Royal Academy to earn his living not as a painter but as an engraver. He remained largely self-taught, but his lack of formal education did not hinder him. Indeed, it may have helped him to become the outstanding imaginative painter of his time and one of the most original poets England has produced.

While working as a jobbing engraver in London, Blake gradually began to establish himself. He married in 1782 Catherine Sophia Boucher. The illiterate daughter of a Battersea market-gardener, she developed into an intelligent and sensitive woman, 'like a flame of many colours of precious jewels' (801)*. She helped Blake with his work, proved a firm companion in troubled times, and tolerated his eccentric ways: 'I have very little of Mr Blake's company; he is always in Paradise', she once declared.[5] They had no children, but this did not prevent him feeling all the concern of a parent for a child misused. When on one occasion he saw a circus boy with a log tied to his foot, Blake's blood boiled and he insisted angrily that the boy should be released.

On his father's death, Blake opened a print shop with his brother Robert in 1784. He also began to do work for the radical publisher Joseph Johnson, at whose house he met some of the leading dissenting intellectuals of the day, including the scientist Joseph Priestley, the philosopher Richard Price, the artist Henry Fuseli, the feminist Mary Wollstonecraft, and the international

---

* All quotations are taken from *Blake: Complete Writings*, ed. Geoffrey Keynes (Oxford University Press, 1972). The number given in brackets after each quotation refers to the page number in this edition.

revolutionary Tom Paine. He also became acquainted with other artists such as Thomas Stothard, John Flaxman, and James Barry. But the hoped-for recognition and security eluded him. His first published work *Poetical Sketches* (1783) hardly caused a ripple.

While Blake was trying to establish himself, he followed political developments closely. He passionately supported the American Revolution, and when the French Revolution broke out in 1789 he shared the wild enthusiasm of Godwin and Wordsworth. He sported a *bonnet rouge*, the red liberty cap, in a show of solidarity with the French revolutionaries. On hearing of the persecution of the second part of the *Rights of Man* in 1792, he allegedly helped Thomas Paine escape to France. But when the revolution entered its authoritarian phase with the rise to power of Robespierre and the Terror which followed, he began to have doubts. When Britain declared war on revolutionary France in 1794, he despaired.

The French Revolution was clearly a turning point in Blake's life. In the period of reaction which followed, Blake witnessed the government repression of radicals, the censorship of the 'Gagging Acts', and the anger of the Church and King mobs who were ready to ransack libraries and throw the disaffected artist or poet in the mud. Blake was obliged to clothe his radical message with allegorical garments. But he never retreated into an ethereal world of the imagination or turned his back on politics in the broadest sense.

Blake had moved to Lambeth in 1790. He lived at Hercules Buildings which had a small garden with an unpruned vine. In a summerhouse, he used to sit naked with Catherine; discovered one day reciting passages from Milton's *Paradise Lost* together, Blake cried: '"Come in! It's only Adam and Eve, you know!"'[6] Whether true or not, the anecdote is certainly in keeping with Blake's sentiments; he rejected original sin, glorified in the naked body, advocated the free satisfaction of physical desire, and loved Milton and Catherine. He wrote at the time: 'The nakedness of woman is the work of God' (152). And he was not embarrassed to witness it.

Blake's stay at Lambeth proved one of the most prosperous and creative periods in his life. But his happiness was never complete. Partly perhaps because of the physical exhaustion which followed moments of creative energy, and partly because he feared for his own life in the growing political reaction, he wrote in a notebook in June 1793: 'I say I shan't live five years, And if I live one it will be a Wonder' (187). Things went from bad to worse. His major first commission for a large book of his own designs, Young's *Night Thoughts*, completed when he was nearly forty, was published in the slump of 1797. Although a superb series of coloured illustrations, it failed. In addition to his growing sense of failure and the worsening political situation, he seems to have been constitutionally prey to depression. In July 1800, he admitted to a friend that he had only just begun to emerge from 'a Deep pit of Melancholy, Melancholy without any real reason for it, a Disease which God keep you from & all good men' (798).

Although he had to rely on the support of his friends, especially Thomas Butts, Blake increasingly wanted to be his own man. In 1799, he wrote to a possible client: 'I find more & more that my Style of Designing is a Species by itself, & in this which I send you have been compell'd by my Genius or Angel to follow where he led; if I were to act otherwise it would not fulfill the purpose for which alone I live, which is... to renew the lost Art of the Greeks' (791-2). But it did not mean that Blake wanted to turn his back on the world; he just happened to see it differently from most other people:

> I feel that a Man may be happy in This World. And I know that This World Is a World of imagination & Vision. I see Every thing I paint In This World, but Every body does not see alike. To the Eyes of a Miser a Guinea is more beautiful than the Sun, & a bag worn with the use of Money has more beautiful proportions than a Vine filled with Grapes. The tree which moves some to tears of joy is in the Eyes of others only a Green thing that stands in the way. Some See Nature all Ridicule & Deformity, & by these I shall not regulate my proportions; & Some Scarce see Nature at all. But to the Eyes of the Man of Imagination, Nature is Imagination itself. As a man is, So he Sees. (793)

At the turn of the century, John Flaxman introduced Blake to the mediocre poet William Hayley who began commissioning work from Blake. Hayley was living on the Sussex coast. Eager for a change, Blake decided to go and live near him. He rented a small cottage in Felpham, a small seaside village next to Bognor. Blake and Catherine were happy to breathe fresh sea air and take in the wide sweep of the bay. He soon experienced his first 'Vision of Light' (804) sitting on the yellow sands and went on to write some of his most beautiful lyrics. But it was not to last. Blake's spiritual state troubled him: 'I am under the direction of Messengers from Heaven, Daily & Nightly; but the nature of such things is not, as some suppose, without trouble or care' (812).

Hayley continued to give him some engraving work but with his own work unappreciated or misunderstood, it was galling for Blake to have to toil for his poetic inferiors. He had to grapple with ill-health and penury. But not all was gloom: 'We are very Happy sitting at tea by a wood fire in our Cottage, the wind singing above our roof & the sea roaring at a distance, but if sickness comes all is unpleasant' (820), he wrote in January 1803.

This was only a temporary respite. Even in his little garden in Felpham he could not be free: one John Scholfield, a soldier of the King, rudely disturbed his fragile peace in the following August. When Blake forcibly turned him out of his garden, the soldier brought a charge against him for assault and for uttering seditious and treasonable expressions. Blake allegedly said 'damn the King' and 'all you Soldiers are sold for Slaves'.[7] Blake was cleared at the assizes in Chichester, but it was a close shave and it shook his nerves.

He decided in the autumn to return to London but the interest of his contemporaries continued to evade him. Although there was a demand for engravers, Blake found it increasingly difficult to find work. A show of his paintings in 1809, his last great effort to win recognition, failed. He fell out with many of his fellow craftsmen and most people who knew of his poetry and painting felt that they were incomprehensible, if not insane.

Yet he continued to take an active interest in social and political events, commenting perceptively in his letters on relations with France, slavery, the Poor Laws, the struggle in London between journeymen printers and their masters, industry, commerce and culture. His inspiration never left him: 'excuse my enthusiasm or rather madness,' he wrote to Hayley in 1804, 'for I am really drunk with intellectual vision whenever I take a pencil or graver into my hand, even as I used to be in my youth, and as I have not been for twenty dark, but very profitable, years' (852). Despite his difficulties, when he was nearly seventy he produced his magnificent *Illustrations to the Book of Job* (1826) which showed him at the height of his imaginative powers. Towards the end of his life, the painter John Linnell came to his aid and he attracted a small group of enthusiasts. They included Samuel Palmer, who likened him to Socrates, and recorded that 'He was a man without a mask; his aim simple, his path straight forwards, and his wants few: so he was free, noble and happy'.[8] Blake died on 12 August 1827, as he had always lived, in obscure poverty. He had the misfortune to have been born in a world wracked by war and industrial change, in a materialistic and cruel age completely out of joint with his own visionary and libertarian impulses.

On the face of it, Blake's life might appear one continual failure. He lived through and had great hopes of the American Revolution and the French Revolution. He witnessed and suffered directly from the triumph of the Industrial Revolution and the failure of British Revolution. Yet he recreated this experience in his poetic and artistic works and drew out their implications for humanity. He may have despaired at times, but he never lost hope. To the end of his life, he demanded a fair price for work and space for the creative imagination. He looked forward to a time when people would live in harmony with each other and nature, released from economic and psychological dependence, and free to develop the full potential of their being.

Tradition

The anarchist thinker Peter Kropotkin once observed: 'Throughout the history of our civilisation, two traditions, two opposing tendencies have confronted each other: the Roman and the Popular; the imperial and the federalist; the authoritarian and the libertarian'.[9] Blake's work bears witness to this struggle and he places himself firmly in the popular and libertarian tradition, rejecting all religious and political domination. He pictured the history of the world and the life of the individual as a constant struggle between authority and liberty, which in his symbolic framework took the opposing forces of Urizen and Los, God and Jesus, Spectre and Emanation. His ultimate goal was to go beyond such contradictions and conflict, to rebuild the Jerusalem of a free society, and to realize the godlike potentiality in humanity. He became an anarchist because he rejected all forms of imposed authority and celebrated freedom both in its negative sense of being free from restraint and in its positive sense of being free to realise one's potential. Indeed, he set no limits to personal liberty: 'No bird soars too high, if he soars with his own wings' (151).

But beyond this broad orientation, the most important influence on Blake's world view was his Protestant background. It was a radical libertarian Protestantism which rejected the repressive aspects of Puritanism. Excluded from public life in Church and State, the Dissenters in Blake's own day formed a separate interest and constituted a permanent undercurrent of social criticism. The Dissenting Interest, as it came to be known, encouraged individualism and self-examination and had an instinctive suspicion of all authority.[10] It pitted the right of private judgement against established beliefs and received opinions. Its culture produced the great radical thinkers Thomas Paine, Richard Price, Joseph Priestley and William Godwin who felt the same enthusiasm as Blake about the outbreak of the French Revolution.

But while sharing the libertarian assumptions of these rational Dissenters, Blake was also in touch with an underground heretical tradition which influenced his thought in a communitarian and chiliastic direction. It finds its roots in the mystical anarchists of the millenarian sects, especially the Brethren of the Free Spirit of the Middle Ages.[11] It re-emerged in the extreme left amongst Anabaptists, Ranters and Diggers of the English Revolution, who wanted to build God's kingdom on earth and live in perfect freedom and complete equality.[12] It continued in the sects like the Muggletonians and Taskites which survived in London in Blake's youth.[13] It was a tradition which expressed social aspirations in Biblical language, which wanted to replace the Babylon of existing Church and State with the Jerusalem of a free society in which people would live according to the Everlasting Gospel of mutual aid and forgiveness. Indeed, Blake was far from alone amongst the radical Dissenters in the 1790s in using the imagery of the Revelation to express his revolutionary aspirations, arguing about the rule of Anti-Christ and hoping for the millennium.[14]

When Blake added to this radical Dissenting tradition what he found in the esoteric tradition of the Cabbala and in the mystical writings of Swedenborg and Boehme, it became a heady and revolutionary brew indeed. But whatever the influences at work on the young Blake, he made them his own. By the use of his creative imagination, he fashioned his own distinctive world view: 'I must Create a System', he wrote, 'or be enslav'd by another Man's. / I will not Reason & Compare: my business is to Create' (629). The result was that where Godwin developed the rationalist tendency within Dissent to anarchist conclusions, Blake elaborated the mystical strand to the same end.

Philosophy

T. S. Eliot, standing in a very different Catholic and monarchial tradition, commented on 'a certain meanness of culture' in Blake's thought and rather disparagingly likened his philosophy to an 'ingenious piece of home made furniture'.[15] Although a largely self-taught thinker and primarily a painter and poet, Blake is more than a philosophical Robinson Crusoe, patching odd and esoteric bits of knowledge together. His philosophy does not creak and sway but has a solid, massive and organic wholeness about it. It is more like a Henry Moore sculpture than a rustic tool. Moreover, it not only questions many fundamental assumptions in moral and political philosophy but threatens the materialist and rationalist premises of Western civilisation itself.

The most striking and decisive aspect about Blake's thought is its dialectical nature. He rejected the mechanical and materialist philosophy which dominated the universities and schools. Like Lao Tse, he saw reality as a constant process of flux and believed that change occurs through the dynamic interplay of opposing forces. Every substance has two inherent qualities which Blake called 'contraries':

> Without Contraries is no progression. Attraction and Repulsion, Reason and Energy, Love and Hate, are necessary to Human existence.
>
> From these contraries spring what the religious call Good & Evil. Good is the passive that obeys Reason. Evil is the active springing from Energy.
>
> Good is Heaven. Evil is Hell. (149)

This conflict between the contraries at the root of all things is not only inevitable but also beneficial; indeed, 'Opposition is true Friendship' (157). The higher synthesis of wisdom moreover can only emerge from the conflict between innocence and experience, good and evil, liberty and authority. Intellectual and corporeal war is therefore an integral part of reality. This dialectical way of looking at things was as essential to Blake's vision as the cornea is to the eye. As his iconoclastic annotations show, he even engaged in a dialectical polemic with the authors he read.

In the end, however, Blake foresees a higher synthesis taking place in the new society of Jerusalem. In personal and historical terms, there comes a marriage of heaven and hell, a reconciliation between mind and body, imagination and reason, conscience and desire, rich and poor, humanity and nature. As in Marx's communist society, Blake believed that at the end of history there would be no longer any antagonism between man and man, and man and nature.

Blake's metaphysics may best be described as a kind of pantheistic idealism. He rejected the rationalism of Newton, the empiricism of Bacon, and the sensationalism of Locke which presented the external world as matter in motion governed by universal laws. For them, the world consisted of a finite quantity to be weighed and measured and classified. Blake was convinced that their mechanical philosophy, which shaped the dominant world view at the time, made the cardinal error of separating the perceiving mind from the object of perception, the observer from the observed.

Blake, on the other hand, was a philosophical idealist, believing that the world is not made of matter but of organized spirit. The everyday world of apparent permanence and stability presented to the senses is illusionary but not the spiritual and visionary:

> A Spirit and a Vision are not, as the modern philosophy supposes, a cloudy vapour, or a nothing: they are organised and minutely articulated beyond all that the mortal and perishing nature can produce. He who does not imagine in stronger and better lineaments, and in stronger and better light than his perishing, mortal eye can see, does not imagine at all. (576)

For Blake, there is no difference between the observer and the observed for all things exist in the imagination: 'To Me This World is all One continued Vision or Fancy or Imagination' (793). Since all natural phenomena only exist in consciousness, it follows that a person's perceptual apparatus will determine what he perceives: 'As a man is, So he Sees' (793).

At the same time, Blake believes that the independent and separate existence of the physical world is ultimately a delusion. Like the contemporary Platonist Thomas Taylor, he distinguishes between this fleeting world of time and space presented to the senses and an eternal and unchanging world perceived by the imagination: 'Accident ever varies, Substance can never suffer change nor decay' (589). This 'Vegetable Universe', as Blake calls it, is thus 'a faint shadow' of the real and eternal world. It is the purpose of the artist, he believes, to use the 'Divine Arts of Imagination' to depict this real world, depicting purer forms than those perceived by the mortal eye (716-17).

Blake was also a nominalist, in that he believed that there are no universals or general terms but only particulars: 'Every class is Individual' (460). This had important corollaries for his art, morality and politics. In the first place, he hated the kind of generalised nature Joshua Reynolds tried to portray and insisted that the artist should see nature in terms of minute particulars: 'To Generalize is to be an Idiot. To Particularize is the Alone Distinction of Merit' (451). This approach was central to Blake's way of seeing the world. Some of his most beautiful images are of the minute objects in nature: wild thyme, meadowsweet, the pebble, the clod of clay, the ant, and the grasshopper. In addition, Blake's nominalism led him in the sphere of ethics and politics to anarchist conclusions. Like Godwin, he believed that every case should be considered a rule unto itself. As a result, he went on to reject all moral rules and man-made laws.

Nature

Blake's concept of nature follows from his dialectical and idealist position. On the one hand, he stresses that 'Nature Teaches us nothing of Spiritual Life but only of Natural Life' (412). The science which only studies nature is therefore the 'Tree of Death' (777). But Blake here is only talking of Newton's nature, the nature of matter in motion. If we accept that 'Nature is Imagination itself' (793), then the 'sweet Science' (379) of true knowledge is possible. Like modern ecologists, Blake adopted a holistic approach to nature, stressing its interdependence, its unity in diversity, and its organic growth. If we go beyond our five senses, if the doors of perception are cleansed, then we will see that 'every thing that lives is Holy' (160).

Human beings are not separate from nature like subject and object, but an integral part of it. Unfortunately, utilitarian and exploitative man has interfered with the beneficial course of nature: 'The Bible says that God formed Nature perfect', Blake wrote, 'but that Man perverted the order of Nature, since which time the Elements are fill'd with the Prince of Evil' (388). Men in their fallen state have therefore introduced self-interest and cruelty into the originally pure natural order. But this is not true of all men; a few like Blake are horrified by the callous treatment of other species. In *Auguries of Innocence*, he makes one of the most eloquent pleas for animal rights ever made:

> A Robin Red breast in a Cage
> Puts all Heaven in a Rage.
> A dove house fill'd with doves & Pigeons
> Shudders Hell thro' all its regions.
> A dog starv'd at his Master's Gate
> Predicts the ruin of the State.
> A Horse misus'd upon the Road
> Calls to Heaven for Human blood.
> Each outcry of the hunted Hare
> A fibre from the Brain does tear.
> A Skylark wounded in the wing,
> A Cherubim does cease to sing.
> The Game Cock clip'd & arm'd for fight
> Does the Rising Sun affright.
> Every Wolf's & Lion's howl
> Raises from Hell a Human Soul.
> The wild deer, wand'ring here & there,
> Keeps the Human Soul from Care.
> The Lamb misus'd breeds Public strife
> And yet forgives the Butcher's Knife.   (431)

Further along the chain of being, Blake sees plants and objects as having a spiritual and aesthetic quality. In his poems, clods of mud and pebbles talk, flowers feel. Blake's profound ecological sensibility also comes through in his letters where he laments the fact that in this fallen world dominated by the cash nexus to the eyes of a miser 'a Guinea is more beautiful than the Sun, & a bag worn with the use of Money has more beautiful proportions than a Vine filled with Grapes. The tree which moves some to tears of joy is in the Eyes of others only a Green thing that stands in the way' (793). Blake speaks directly to those modern ecologists who argue that a forest cannot be merely seen in terms of an economic unit but as an integral part of the earth's ecosystem which nurtures animal life as well as the human spirit. When the sun rises, Blake did not see a round disk like a guinea but 'an Innumerable company of the Heavenly host crying "Holy, Holy, Holy is the Lord God Almighty"' (617). He was one of those people who are able:

> To see a World in a Grain of Sand
> And a Heaven in a Wild Flower,
> Hold Infinity in the palm of your hand
> And Eternity in an hour. (431)

Human Nature

The human species finds its place within the organic world of nature, but it is the most important species: 'Where man is not, nature is barren' (152). Humanity is unique in that it is made in God's image, the Divine image. Like the Christian anarchist Tolstoy, Blake believes that the kingdom of God is within us: 'All deities reside in the human breast' (153). There is no distinction between the creator and the created: 'God is Man & exists in us & we in him' (775). Man is thus primarily a spiritual thing and is not bound by his physical body: 'Spirits are organized men' (577). Blake calls this spiritual human essence the 'Imagination' or 'Poetic Genius' and insists that the 'Poetic Genius is the true Man, and that the body or outward form of Man is derived from the Poetic Genius' (98). At the same time, Blake does not fall back on traditional dualism, separating the mind from the body, praising the one to the detriment of the other. He remains a thoroughgoing monist idealist.

Body and mind are two aspects of a common spirit. The body is not only organised spirit but also the source of creative energy:

1. Man has no Body distinct from his Soul; for that call'd Body is a portion of Soul discern'd by the five Senses, the chief inlets of Soul in this age.
2. Energy is the only life, and is from the Body; and Reason is the bound or outward circumference of Energy.
3. Energy is Eternal Delight. (149)

Blake thus sees the unconscious and instinctual side of our make-up as a positive driving force. And like Godwin who defines the will as the last act of the understanding, Blake insists 'Thought is Act' (400).

Blake calls the human essence the 'Imagination' but he also celebrates imagination as the most important creative faculty within us. Indeed, his theory of the imagination in which inspiration is contrasted with memory recalls Coleridge's distinction between Imagination and Fancy. At the same time, Blake is highly critical of the faculty of reason: 'Man by his reasoning power can only compare & judge of what he has already perciev'd' (97). But it would be wrong to conclude that Blake is irrational or anti-intellectual. He does not reject reason out of hand, but only that kind of reason which controls the passions and serves self-interest: 'He who sees the Ratio only, sees himself only' (98). Reason, in Blake's mythology, becomes Urizen, the 'horizon', and is presented as a burdened, entangled, listless tyrant. Blake hates the kind of instrumental and analytical reason which can destroy what it dissects and which argues that ends justifies means. He abhors the reason which acts as 'an Abstract objecting power that Negatives every thing' (629). On its own, naked reason can only curb, govern and destroy:

> The Spectre is the Reasoning Power in Man, & when separated
> From Imagination and closing itself as in steel in a Ratio
> Of the Things of Memory, It thence frames Law & Moralities

> To destroy Imagination, the Divine Body, by Martyrdoms
> & Wars. (714)

But Blake here is only talking about analytical and instrumental reason. It is the task of naked reason to recognise its own inadequacy, not to abolish itself entirely. Moreover, Blake makes no crude distinction between reason and the passions 'For a Tear is an Intellectual Thing', as well as an emotional one. If the understanding encourages the passions rather than curbs them, then the 'Treasures of Heaven' can be 'Realities of Intellect' (615).

In Blake's psychology, the whole person is made up of four essential components which he calls the Four Zoas: body (Tharmas), reason (Urizen), emotion (Luvah), and spirit (Urthona). Blake does not suggest that one should exist without the other. Love, for instance, involves physical, intellectual and emotional states, but in true sexuality the spiritual is needed to perfect the physical. Moreover, to achieve a state of heightened consciousness, to obtain full visionary awareness, it is necessary to reconcile energy, reason, emotion and spirit. In his scheme of things, Blake calls this a 'fourfold vision'.

On the first level of consciousness, mechanical reason holds sway in darkness (which Blake calls heaven). The second level, associated with fire, is the realm of energy (hell). The third is a state of light which unites the first two into *The Marriage of Heaven and Hell*, as Blake's prose-poem puts it. The fourfold vision is the inspired state of full light which brings together all the other levels of consciousness:

> Now I a fourfold vision see,
> And a fourfold vision is given to me;
> 'Tis fourfold in my supreme delight
> And threefold in soft Beaulah's night
> And twofold Always. May God us keep
> From Single vision & Newton's sleep! (818)

Beaulah is the country in Bunyan from which the pilgrims can see the city they are searching for.

Unlike other contemporary radicals, Blake believed in innate

I. Newton measuring the Ratio (1795)
(By permission of the Tate Gallery, London)

ideas. Writing against Reynolds, he maintained that we are born with a sense of ideal beauty and a moral conscience: 'Innate Ideas are in Every Man, Born with him; they are truly Himself (459). Where Godwin and Paine argued that we are products of our circumstances, Blake insisted that intelligence is genetic: 'The Man who says that the Genius is not Born, but Taught – Is a Knave' (470). Indeed, nothing important is acquired in a person's make-up for he brings all that he has into the world with him: 'Man is Born Like a Garden ready Planted & Sown' (471).

Unfortunately, the growing child can forget his innate knowledge as he becomes lost in the cave of the five senses. The grown adult, absorbed in external nature, easily becomes cut off from his or her innate universal ground. For this reason, Blake believes that children who have not had their visions clouded by sensuous infatuation and worldly interest, are more capable of appreciating and elucidating his visions.

Although we have an innate moral sense or conscience that we can rely upon as the 'voice of God' (385), it is no easy task to adopt the right course of action. Within all of us, there is a constant struggle between our good or bad side, between our Emanation and Spectre. The Spectre represents for Blake everything that is negative in the world: tyranny, empire, false reason, conventional religion, and self-hood. It is associated with the Jehovah God of the Old Testament. The Emanation on the other hand stands for all that is positive: creative energy, imagination, forgiveness, and Jesus. The struggle between the two forces takes the form of corporeal and mental war.

> My Spectre around me night & day
> Like a Wild beast guards my way.
> My Emanation far within
> Weeps incessantly for my Sin. (415)

Nevertheless, the conflict between the forces of good and evil are not eternal as in the Manichean universe. Good can triumph over evil, the Emanation can defeat the Spectre when the individual realises his or her divine potential:

> Each man is his Spectre's power
> Untill the arrival of that hour
> When his Humanity awake
> And cast his own Spectre into the Lake.   (421)

Out of this dialectical struggle between the Spectre and Emanation should emerge the higher synthesis of Divine Humanity which will reconcile all the opposing forces. This is the ultimate goal of Blake's visionary humanism which insists: 'The worship of God is: Honouring his gifts in other men, each according to his genius, and loving the greatest men best: those who envy or calumniate great men hate God; for there is no other God.' (158)

Blake's contemporary radicals like Paine and Godwin rejected the notion of innate ideas since they believed that it could be used to justify social inequality. Blake however felt that a belief in innate intelligence offered no grounds for social discrimination. Not everyone is born a genius, but for Blake every one is equally made in the divine image and has a divine potential. This led Blake to talk in terms of Universal Humanity while recognizing local differences: 'As all men are alike (tho' infinitely various), So all Religions &, as all similars, have one source' (98).

While the lawyers of the French Revolution were only prepared to extend political rights to property-owning white males, Blake made an impassioned plea for racial and sexual equality. He deplored slavery and knew of its cruelties directly. He depicted the horrors of the slave trade for his antislaver friend Stedman and was so horrified by his drawing of the 'A Negro on the Rack' (1796), that he left it unsigned. He thought the African as capable as the European of spiritual enlightenment and social freedom. In 'A Song of Liberty', Blake calls on the citizen of London 'enlarge thy countenance!' and exclaims: 'O African! black African! (go, winged thought, widen his forehead)' (159). In a 'Little Black Boy', Blake at first seems to link the black and white boys with good and bad angels, but he goes beyond this moral dualism by presenting the black boy as teaching the white:

> When I from black and he from white cloud free,
> And round the tent of God like lambs we joy,
>
> I'll shade him from the heat, till he can bear
> To lean in joy upon our father's knee;
> And then I'll stand and stroke his silver hair,
> And be like him, and he will then love me. (125)

Colour is therefore superficial and unimportant: black and white skins are merely the outward appearance of the physical bodies of children which will eventually vanish like clouds.[16]

When it comes to sexual equality, Blake's position might at first sight appear more ambivalent. On the one hand, he saw like his friend Mary Wollstonecraft that women were enslaved in the institution of marriage as the slave was enthralled in the plantation, and that loveless marriage is no different from prostitution. Blake and Wollstonecraft not only collaborated together – he illustrated her *Original Stories from Real Life* (1788) – but were also close friends. At the end of her novel *Mary* (1788) the heroine longs to enter that 'world *where there is neither marrying*, nor giving in marriage'.[17] Many years later Blake echoed her sentiments in *Jerusalem* where Albion tells Vala 'In Eternity they neither marry nor are given in marriage' (660). In the *Visions of the Daughters* of Albion (1793), he condemns the cruel absurdity of enforced chastity and marriage without love:

> Till she who burns with youth, and knows no fixed lot, is bound
> In spells of law to one she loathes? and must she drag the chain
> Of life in weary lust? must chilling, murderous thoughts obscure
> The clear heaven of her eternal spring; to bear the wintry rage
> Of a harsh terror, driv'n to madness, bound to hold a rod
> Over her shrinking shoulders all the day, & all the night
> To turn the wheel of false desire, and longings that wake her womb

II. *Bromion & Oothoon chained at the mouth of a cave, frontispiece of*
Visions of the Daughters of Albion *(1793)*
(By pemission of the Trustees of the British Museum, London)

> To the abhorred birth of cherubs in the human form,
> That live a pestilence & die a meteor, & are no more... (193)

To end this state of affairs, Blake calls for an end to patriarchical possessiveness and defends the right of women to complete self-fulfilment.

Nevertheless, while Blake advocates 'Love! Love! Love! happy happy Love! free as the mountain wind!', a degree of ambivalence arises when he describes such freedom in terms of constraint: 'silken nets and traps of adamant will Oothoon spread' to catch 'girls of mild silver, or of furious gold'.[18] Is he suggesting that Oothoon should supply her lover with girls so that she can watch them in 'happy copulation' on a bank and draw the 'pleasures of this free born joy'? (194) Or is he referring symbolically to instincts which should not be mutually exclusive? Again, although Blake clearly loved his companion Catherine deeply, she acted as if her chief role was to be his supporter and handmaiden.

In the prophetic books, Blake also often presents the female figure in the traditional role of the cunning temptress or the passionate destroyer. Los's female Emanation, in the guise of Enitharmon, is opposed to the imagination, embodying both the indulgence and repression of the passions. She comforts Los but also emasculates him. However, this is only half the story. Later in the guise of Jerusalem, the Emanation of Albion, woman represents liberty, the desire to unite with Jesus, and becomes one with Albion.

Blake in reality thought that the male and female principles are not separate and lodged in bodies of different genders, but are within us all: when Enitharmon is divided from Los, for instance, man becomes divided and jealousy comes into being. Ultimately, Blake believed that sex belongs only to the divided world of time and space: true 'Humanity knows not of Sex' (656) and 'Humanity is far above / Sexual organization' (721). In this, he accepted Boehme's doctrine that the Eternal Man is androgynous.[19]

Politics

Blake's politics are not presented as a coherent system or in a consistent manner. He had a very low opinion of traditional political philosophy, associating it with the mechanical and utilitarian mind of John Locke whose defence of government as the protector of private property had become the dominant Whig ideology. Blake even put down the wretched state of the arts in Europe directly to the 'wretched State of Political Science, which is the Science of Sciences' (600).

It has been suggested that Blake came to despair of politics after his trial for sedition at the turn of the century[20] Certainly, he wrote around 1810 'I am really sorry to see my Countrymen trouble themselves about Politics' (600). Yet Blake only despaired of politics in its conventional sense of factions and parties jockeying for power. His position can be called anti-political only if politics is defined in its narrow sense of the art of government. Blake was not frightened from politics but he reached the anarchist conclusion that conventional politics in the form of governments are a denial of life and an insuperable bar to human freedom.

Blake never rejected politics in the broader sense of the relationships between human beings in society. His political views are not presented in isolation for they form an inseparable part of his religious thought: 'Are not Religion & Politics the Same Thing?', he asked, adding 'Brotherhood is Religion' (689). And just as his political and religious beliefs are intertwined, so they are both in turn based on his particular view of nature, society, and the self.

There is a critical and a constructive dimension to Blake's politics. He offered both a devastating critique of existing society and a powerful alternative vision of a free society. Although he pictured transformed humanity living in the new society of Jerusalem in the future, he drew inspiration from the mythical past. Like the Brethren of the Free Spirit, the Diggers and the Ranters whom he resembles so closely, he wished to restore humanity to its original state. He assumed like them that in the Garden of

Eden man and woman lived in a state of innocence and wholeness, without private property, class distinctions and human authority: 'When Adam delved and Eve span, who was then the Gentleman?'. Indeed, Blake seems to have felt that 'The Primeval State of Man was Wisdom, Art and Science' (621). After the Fall, men and women were condemned to toil, poverty and suffering. They became weighed down by positive institutions, mangled by Church and State, oppressed by Lord and King. As private property developed, and the State was established to defend it, people became divided against each other and classes came into direct conflict. With the loss of human innocence, experience thus created a world of contradictions, between Man and Nature, State and Society, Capital and Labour, Church and Christianity.

As always with Blake, there is a close parallel between psychology and politics: the state of the individual reflects the state of the society in which he lives. Within man himself, a conflict developed between reason and imagination, conscience and desire, body and soul. The sleeping soul fell into 'its deadly dreams of Good & Evil when it leaves Paradise following the Serpent' (614). But this state of affairs is not inevitable. Revolutionary energy is also at work in the individual and history and can transform things as they have become.

Blake saw it his express purpose to try and recreate the lost age of innocence and freedom which he supposed had once existed at the beginning of time. 'The Nature of my Work is Visionary or Imaginative', he wrote. 'It is an Endeavour to Restore what the Ancients called the Golden Age'. But in the fallen world of experience it is impossible to go back to an original state of innocence; the only way is forward to create the whole person in a new society in a higher synthesis of innocence and experience. In *The Book of Thel* (1789), Blake implies that when the virgin hears of the dangers to which her own five senses will expose her, she is wrong to fear the world of experience and withdraw. There can be no genuine innocence which has not been tested by knowledge of the world since 'Innocence dwells with Wisdom, but never with Ignorance' (380).

Blake lived in an age of revolution and like most of his fellow radicals experienced the extremes of hope and disappointment. He lived at a time when the Nation State in Britain oppressed and exploited the people which came under its sway both at home and in the colonies in India and America. He witnessed the Industrial Revolution which not only threatened his craft as an engraver but was turning England's green and pleasant land into a polluted desert of dark satanic mills. In the new cities, he saw 'turrets & towers & domes / Whose smoke destroy'd the pleasant gardens, & whose running kennels / Chok'd the bright rivers' (361). To the north, the new factories of England belched smoke and fire and consumed workers; from the south came the din of revolutionary war and the stench of rotting corpses on the battlefields of Europe.

And yet as a boy, Blake had been thrilled by the news of the American Revolution, and as a young man had greeted with wild enthusiasm the French Revolution, convinced that it would inaugurate a new reign of peace, prosperity and freedom on earth. He became deeply disappointed when the Revolution degenerated into the Terror and horrified when Britain went to war with France. In 1800, he recalled how in his life a 'mighty & awful change' threatened the earth and despaired how it ended in war:

> The American War began. All its dark horrors passed
>   before my face
> Across the Atlantic to France. Then the French Revolution
>   commenc'd in thick clouds,
> And My Angels have told me that seeing such visions
>   I could not subsist on the Earth ... (799)

But Blake never lost in his darkest moments his vision of a free society which the two revolutions had inspired. While most of his radical contemporaries went over to the reaction or fell by the wayside, Blake remained with Godwin faithful to his libertarian and egalitarian ideals.

The State

In the critical phase of his political thought, Blake offers a powerful indictment of things as they are. Few writers have made such a profound and telling analysis of political imposture. Political authority is for Blake the principal source of injustice and inequality: 'A Tyrant is the Worst disease & the Cause of all others' (402). It is State structures of power which block access to the divine potential within humanity. Like Godwin and later anarchists, he recognized that the State has an iron grip on society, encouraging the corrupt and wealthy to corrode every aspect of the nation: 'The Whore & Gambler, by the State/Licenc'd, build that Nation's Fate' (433). As the supreme power within a nation, the State is also ultimately based on military might:

> The Strongest Poison ever known
> Came from Caesar's Laurel Crown.
> Nought can deform the Human Race
> Like to the Armour's iron brace.   (433)

Caesar in the radical Protestant tradition was always used as a symbol for the State.

Blake was one of the first to recognize that war is the health of the State. He lived in an era of total war, when the traditional skirmishes between small groups of professionals had been transformed into mass engagements of armies which involved the entire civil population. The Industrial Revolution was further making the instruments of death cheaper and more effective. As early as 1784, Blake showed his disgust with war in a drawing at the Royal Academy entitled 'War Unchained by an Angel – Fire, Pestilence and Famine'. He went on to show that war not only involves aggression against other nations, but enables the State to use violence against its own people. As Britain entered the war against France, Blake wrote that the 'Code of War' caused 'Churches, Hospitals, Castles, Palaces, / Like nets & gins & traps to catch the joys of Eternity' (246). The sick mentality of war moreover distorted the fundamental values of humanity so that 'The Soldier, arm'd with

Sword & Gun, / Palsied strikes the Summer's Sun' (432). With prophetic horror, Blake anticipated the devastation which unchecked power could wreak. In *Vala, or the Four Zoas*, he writes:

> The Villages Lament: they faint, outstretch'd upon
>   the plain.
> Wailing runs round the Valleys from the Mill & from
>   the Barn.
> But most the polish'd Palaces, dark, silent, bow
>   with dread,
> Hiding their books & pictures underneath the dens
>   of Earth.
>
> The Cities send to one another saying: 'My sons are Mad
> 'With wine of cruelty. Let us plat a scourge, O Sister City.'
> Children are nourish'd for the Slaughter; once the Child
>   was fed
> With Milk, but wherefore now are Children fed with
>   blood?   (275)

Blake even seems to predict the nuclear winter which could result from universal war:

> There is no City, nor Cornfield, nor Orchard; all is Rock
>   & Sand.
> There is no Sun, nor Moon, nor Star, but rugged wintry
>   rocks
> Justling together in the void, suspended by inward fires.
>   (276)

Blake's opposition to war was total, and he wished to transform corporeal war into mental war. Although in 1809 he mockingly pictured 'The Spiritual Form of Nelson' as a handsome boy with a halo, it is clear that Blake saw him as an evil force guiding Leviathan 'in whose wreathings are infolded the Nations of the Earth'.[21] To make sure his message was absolutely clear, in his 'Spiritual Form of Pitt guiding Behemoth', Blake presented Pitt as an angel guiding the 'storms of war' and showed Behemoth's belly crammed with crowned kings and howling warriors.

Blake did not think that the State is the only cause of evil. Authority in all its forms is the principal cause. It can exert its destructive sway in the home as much as in parliament, at the head of the table or on the throne. Nevertheless, Blake was closer to Godwin than Paine in his rejection of government 'When the Reverence of Government is Lost', he wrote, 'it is better than when it is found' (401). He was on the side of Christ against Caesar, of the people against the State: 'If Caesar is Right, Christ is Wrong both in Politics & Religion' (396). One of the bitterest calumnies he could think of for the renegade Dr Watson, Bishop of Llandaff, was to describe him as a 'State trickster' (384). Blake agreed moreover with Godwin that there is no such thing as a legitimate social contract; like religious and moral codes, all contracts are the creations of the fallen mind.

Whatever the form political authority took, Blake rejected it. True to his radical Dissenting background, he remained a staunch republican throughout his life. In 1791 while he was composing *The French Revolution* he wrote in his commonplace book not intended for publication:

> "Let the Brothels of Paris be opened
> "With many an alluring dance,
> "To awake the Physicians thro' the city,"
> Said the beautiful Queen of France.
>
> The King awoke on his couch of gold,
> As soon as he heard these tidings told:
> "Arise & come, both fife & drum,
> "And the [Famine] shall eat both crust & crumb..."
>
> Then he swore a great & solemn Oath:
> "To kill the people I am loth,
> "But If they rebel, they must go to hell:
> "They shall have a Priest & a passing bell." (185)

Seven years later, Blake wrote in the margin of his copy of Bacon's *Essays*: 'Every Body hates a King'. In the same work, he also drew a representation of a bottom, labelled: 'The devil's arse'; and hanging from it is a chain of excrement ending in: 'A King' (400). Although he denied the accusation (it might, after all, have cost him his life), he could easily have exclaimed 'damn the King' to the soldier who entered his garden in Felpham in 1803.

What aligns Blake with Godwin and the anarchists is that he saw no remedy for social ills in parliamentary democracy. Where his contemporary radicals like Paine, John Thelwall, and Francis Place all sought to reform parliament, Blake felt that representative government would only curb society and check human creativity: 'Houses of Commons & Houses of Lords appear to me to be fools; they seem to me to be something Else besides Human Life' (600). Blake was not expressing ambivalence or fear about politics here. He had reached the anarchist conclusion that all governments by their very nature perpetuate violence, disorder, and injustice. And just as Godwin felt that government is founded in opinion, and that if a people changed their opinion, a government would have no support, so Blake concluded: 'If Men were Wise, the Most arbitrary Princes could not hurt them' (600).

The State not only claims supreme authority in a given territory, but is also a coercive legal order. Its various branches make, interpret and enforce the laws which it claims are necessary to maintain order. Blake's philosophical position led him to reject all man-made laws. As a nominalist, he felt that no law could be sufficiently general to apply to every individual case: 'One Law for the Lion & Ox is Oppression' (158). As a religious antinomian, he further believed that the moral and ceremonial law is no longer binding on 'God's people' who are in a state of grace; it was a curse resulting from the Fall which need no longer apply.[22] It follows for Blake that all codes which are given under pretence of divine command are 'what Christ pronounced them, The Abomination that maketh desolate' (393). From his own observation and experience, Blake felt no less strongly that laws require prisons to enforce them as much as a repressive morality creates the need for prostitutes: 'Prisons are built with stones of Law, Brothels with bricks of Religion' (151). Indeed, since it is law which alone defines a crime, invites people to commit it, and promises dire punishment, Blake concluded: 'All Penal Laws court Transgression & therefore are cruelty & Murder.' (393)

Blake's criticism of law was as thoroughgoing and radical as Godwin's. Like him, he felt that no law could cover the multitude of individual acts and is thereby inherently unjust. The law moreover appeals to moral and religious principles to justify its policy of revenge and destruction. Referring to 'Albion the punisher & judge', Blake declares:

> He sat by Tyburn's brook, and underneath his heel
>   shot up
> A deadly Tree: he nam'd it Moral Virtue and the Law
> Of God who dwells in Chaos hidden from the human
>   sight. (652)

Like Godwin, Blake believed that law is not the remedy for social disorder and moral chaos, but one of its principal causes.

The Church

Blake's opposition to authority not only led him to reject the State and King, but also the Church and God. Blake's version of Christianity was deeply heretical and he was the first to admit it:

> The Vision of Christ that thou dost see
> Is my Vision's Greatest Enemy:
> Thine has a great hook nose like thine,
> Mine has a snub nose like to mine:
> Thine is a friend of All Mankind,
> Mine speaks in parables to the Blind:
> Thine loves the same world that mine hates,
> Thy Heaven doors are my Hell Gates. (748)

The Hebrew Jehovah of the Old Testament personified for Blake absolute tyranny. In Blake's prophetic writings, he appears as Urizen, the God of Reason who tries to set a limit on the imagination and curb desire. The traditional Christian priest wished to enslave humanity and had caught them in the 'direful web' of organized religion. But Blake felt that the passive and rational Christianity taught by eighteenth-century Deism and Natural Religion was little better. 'The Modern Church', he concluded, 'Crucifies Christ with the Head Downwards' (615). When allied to the State, it created an even more pernicious force for 'State Religion' is the 'source of all Cruelty' (393).

Where the Old Testament God was a tyrant, Blake felt that Jesus Christ had rebelled against his authority in order to help humanity: 'Thinking as I do the Creator of this World is a very Cruel Being, & being a Worshipper of Christ, I cannot help saying: "the Son, O how unlike the Father!" First God Almighty comes with a Thump on the Head. Then Jesus Christ comes with a balm to heal it' (617). In addition, Blake saw Jesus as identifying with the people and attacking the class system which gave political power to the upper classes: 'Did not Jesus descend & become a Servant? The Prince of darkness is a Gentleman & not a Man: he is a Lord Chancellor' (399). In *The Everlasting Gospel* (c.1818), Blake continued to attack the tyrannical God of the Old Testament and presented Jesus as the rebellious son who rejected temporal and divine authority and the ten commandments:

> He scorn'd Earth's Parents, scorn'd Earth's God,
> And mock'd the one & the other's Rod;
> His Seventy Disciples sent
> Against Religion & Government:
> They by the Sword of Justice fell
> And him their Cruel Murderer tell.
> He left his Father's trade to roam
> A wand'ring Vagrant without Home;
> And thus he others' labour stole
> That he might live above Controll.
> The Publicans & Harlots he
> Selected for his Company,
> And from the Adultress turn'd away
> God's righteous Law, that lost its Prey.   (757)

Because Blake believed that Jesus rejected all divine commands and moral laws, he made him the central figure in his mythology and the great liberator in his prophetic writings: 'Jesus was all virtue, and acted from impulse, not from rules' (158). Indeed, for Blake 'The Gospel is Forgiveness of Sins & Has No Moral Precepts' (395).

Mind-Forged Manacles

Blake was no historical materialist but he anticipated Marx in recognizing the power of the ruling ideology to shape the consciousness of the people. He realized just how intimately the modes of consciousness and production are linked. He saw the hegemony of the dominant culture as one of the most powerful forms of slavery: 'mind-forg'd manacles' (216) are as real as iron chains. Blake was thus concerned not only about the mangling influence of political and spiritual authority but also the whole complex superstructure of religion, philosophy, and morality which created chains of illusion.

In philosophy, there was the dominant rationalism of Newton and the empiricism of Locke which made people see only the Ratio and themselves and not the 'Infinite in all things' (98). In religion, the deism of Voltaire and Rousseau had created a natural religion which took no account of the holy and spiritual:

> Mock on, Mock on Voltaire, Rousseau:
> Mock on, Mock on: 'tis all in vain!
> You throw the sand against the wind,
> And the wind blows it back again.
>
> And every sand becomes a Gem
> Reflected in the beams divine;
> Blown back they blind the mocking Eye,
> But still in Israel's paths they shine.   (418)

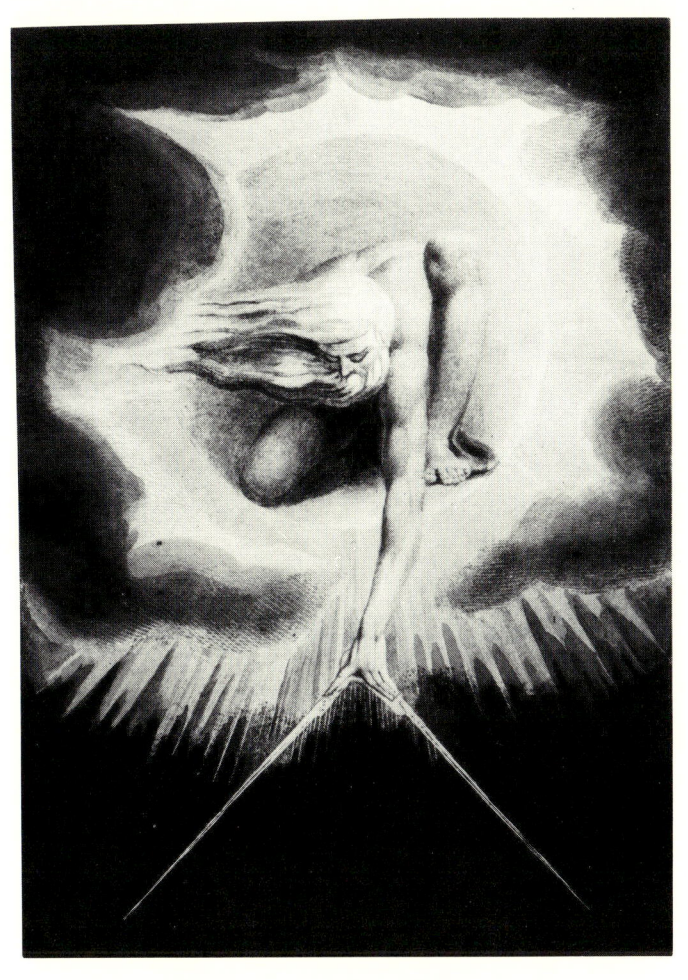

III. *'The Ancient of Days' frontispiece of Europe (1794)*
(By permission of the Trustees of the British Museum)

There were, Blake knew only too well, 'Hirelings in the Camp, the Court & the University, who would, if they could, for ever depress Mental & prolong Corporeal War' (480). In the art world, there were painters, poets and musicians who crept 'into State Government like a catterpiller to destroy' (533). And in education, the young were given a practical training which not only restricted their vision but prepared them to become docile workers in the new factories of the Industrial Revolution:

> I turn my eyes to the Schools & Universities of Europe
> And there behold the Loom of Locke, whose Woof
>   rages dire,
> Wash'd by the Water-wheels of Newton: black the cloth
> In heavy wreathes folds over every Nation: cruel Works
> Of many Wheels I view, wheel without wheel, with cogs
>   tyrannic
> Moving by compulsion each other, not as those in Eden,
>   which,
> Wheel within Wheel, in freedom revolve in harmony &
>   peace.   (636)

Wheels for Blake were symbols of Newton's laws of gravitation which govern and constrain. They were also central pieces of machinery to keep the dark satanic mills rolling.

Above all, Blake was concerned with the corrupting and repressive morality which the unholy alliance of State and Church had imposed on humanity. Together they had encouraged a moral code of deception, deceit, hypocrisy, self-interest, pity and cruelty. This comes clearly through in his *Songs of Experience* where the laughing and joyous children of the *Songs of Innocence* have been abandoned in a cold and miserable world. Caring elders have become cruel taskmasters. In 'The Garden of Love', a Chapel is built on the echoing green and natural instincts are crushed:

> I went to the Garden of Love,
> And saw what I never had seen:
> A Chapel was built in the midst,
> Where I used to play on the green.

> And the gates of this Chapel were shut,
> And "Thou shalt not" writ over the door;
> So I turn'd to the Garden of Love
> That so many sweet flowers bore;
>
> And I saw it was filled with graves,
> And tomb-stones where flowers should be;
> And Priests in black gowns were walking their rounds,
> And binding with briars my joys & desires.   (215)

In this world of experience, the parents of 'The Chimney Sweeper' have gone 'to praise God & his Priest & King / Who make up a heaven of our misery' (212). Indeed, as Blake makes clear in *The Marriage of Heaven and Hell*: 'As the catterpiller chooses the fairest leaves to lay her eggs on, so the priest lays his curse on the fairest joys' (152).

Like the Brethren of the Free Spirit, Blake thought that for the pure in spirit every act is pure.[23] Unlike them, however, he did not restrict his teaching to a small elite, for he believed that the natural desires of all people are positive and healthy. He not only recognized the claims of the unconscious and instinctive side of our make-up, but valued energy above all else – 'Energy is Eternal Delight' (149). For Blake, any thing which hinders action is vicious; his principal criticism of reason is that it tries to bind energy. He even defined murder and theft as 'Hindering Another' (88). The good therefore are not those who try and repress the passions; indeed, according to Blake those who are cast out of heaven are 'All Those who, having no Passions of their own because No Intellect, Have spent their lives in Curbing & Governing other People's by the various arts of Poverty & Cruelty of all kinds. Wo, Wo, Wo to you Hypocrites' (615).

But Blake did not leave it at that. He anticipated Wilhelm Reich in seeing the close link between repression and aggression: war, he suggested, is 'energy Enslav'd' (361). This profound insight is at the centre of Blake's demonic wisdom in *The Marriage of Heaven and Hell*. When Blake writes: 'Sooner murder an infant in its cradle than nurse unacted desires' (152), he means that repressed desires can make a person permanently cruel and destructive. According to Blake, 'He who desires but acts not, breeds pestilence' (151). It is in this symbolic sense that Blake once admitted that he had committed many murders.[24] It follows that spontaneous anger is better than tamed reason: 'The tygers of wrath are wiser than the horses of instruction' (152). As Blake suggests in 'A Poison Tree', if we hold back our anger it can bear strange fruit:

> I was angry with my friend:
> I told my wrath, my wrath did end.
> I was angry with my foe:
> I told it not, my wrath did grow.
>
> And I water'd it in fears,
> Night & morning with my tears;
> And I sunned it with smiles,
> And with soft deceitful wiles.
>
> And it grew both day and night,
> Till it bore an apple bright;
> And my foe beheld it shine,
> And he knew that it was mine,
>
> And into my garden stole
> When the night had veil'd the pole:
> In the morning glad I see
> My foe outstretch'd beneath the tree. (218)

Just as to inhibit action is vicious, so its opposite is true: all act is virtue. It is for this reason that 'Excess in Youth is Necessary to Life' (408). Above all, Blake applied this to sexual desire:

> In a wife I would desire
> What in whores is always found –
> The lineaments of Gratified desire.
>
> Abstinence sows sand all over
> The ruddy limbs & flaming hair,
> But Desire Gratified
> Plants fruits of life & beauty there. (178)

IV. 'Aged Ignorance' For Children: The Gates of Paradise (1793)
(By permission of the Trustees of the British Museum)

Blake did not give sex a 'very modest place in the order of things'; on the contrary, he acknowledged the central importance of libido in psychic life.[25] He not only prefigured Nietzsche in recognizing the subversive nature of energy, but called like Reich for a sexual and political revolution which would release infinite desire. He advocated free love and entertained the idea of a community of women. Blake's alleged mysticism is not therefore timeless and abstract; it implies and involves sensual pleasure. Indeed for Blake, there is no separation between mind and body, intellect and will, for 'Thought is Act' (400).

Existing Society

Blake has left one of the most damning pictures of the Britain of his time which Edmund Burke called an age 'of sophisters, economists, and calculators'.[26] The capitalist drive for profit had not only fired the Industrial Revolution but had led to the imperial conquests in America and India. But Blake suggested that the new breed of capitalists would become their own grave-diggers for 'Empires flourish till they become Commercial, & then they are scatter'd abroad to the four winds' (594). Where Paine saw beneficial results coming in the long run from commerce, Blake thought that it was destructive of both Arts and Empire (593). He saw an excessive concern with money is also disastrous to the soul, turning a person into a miser who would only see a guinea in the setting sun. Blake believed that 'For every Pleasure Money Is Useless' (777). At the same time, he did not celebrate voluntary poverty – poverty, he insisted, is the 'Fool's Rod' (612) – and wanted 'a Fair Price & proportionate Value & General Demand' for his work (446). Ultimately, he dreamed of a moneyless world where all would receive according to their need: 'Give us the Bread that is our due & Right, by taking away Money, or a Price, or Tax upon what is Common to all in thy Kingdom' (788).

Blake earned his living as an artisan and witnessed the onset of the Industrial Revolution. It not only reduced people to cogs and wheels in the new factory system, but darkened England's green and pleasant land. He shared the hostility of the artisans to the new technology which was making their skills obsolete and promised to make them the slaves of the machines. He saw workers in the factories alienated from nature, from each other and from the product of their labour. The new division of labour further divided mind and body, mental and physical work, and exercised only part of the whole personality. As a result, the 'Divine Image' within humanity had been distorted to such an extent that it often appeared to Blake that:

> Cruelty has a Human Heart,
> And Jealousy a Human Face;
> Terror the Human Form Divine,
> And Secrecy the Human Dress.
>
> The Human Dress is forged Iron,
> The Human Form a fiery Forge,
> The Human Face a Furnace seal'd,
> The Human Heart its hungry Gorge. (221)

The effect of industrialization had made the nation become increasingly divided between rich and poor, town and country. Blake did not talk in proto-Marxist terms of capitalists and workers, but he recognized the growing class divisions in society. He spoke of the rich and the poor and acknowledged that there was an emerging 'Middle Class' (406). He consistently aligned himself with the 'People' (403).

Living in London, the first city in Europe with three-quarters of a million inhabitants, Blake saw at first hand the effects of class conflict. In 'London', his most moving short poem, the metropolis appears as a city of lost innocence:

> I wander thro' each charter'd street,
> Near where the charter'd Thames does flow,
> And mark in every face I meet
> Marks of weakness, marks of woe.
>
> In every cry of every Man,
> In every Infant's cry of fear,
> In every voice, in every ban,
> The mind-forg'd manacles I hear.
>
> How the Chimney-sweeper's cry
> Every black'ning Church appalls;
> And the hapless Soldier's sigh
> Runs in blood down Palace walls.
>
> But most thro' midnight streets I hear
> How the youthful Harlot's curse
> Blasts the new born Infant's tear,
> And blights with plagues the Marriage hearse. (216)

The streets and the Thames have become 'charter'd' ('dirty' in an earlier draft) which is associated with cheating and profiteering. Its citizens are gripped by the 'mind-forg'd manacles' of self-interest, hypocrisy, and deceit. The Church is indifferent to the suffering of the workers and the Monarchy is directly responsible for war: 'the hapless Soldier's sigh / Runs in blood down Palace walls'. The institution of loveless marriage is not only linked with prostitution but also with death. The whole poem is indignant about the State institutions of repression which endorse a heartless and acquisitive morality. But while Blake depicts life as hell, he is describing London from within, as a particular human condition not a universal one.[27] As Blake asks in 'Holy Thursday', when paltry alms were distributed by the Church:

> Is this a holy thing to see
> In a rich and fruitful land
> Babes reduc'd to misery,
> Fed with cold and usurous hand? (211)

But Blake did not restrict his vision only to London or even England. In Europe in 1794, the whole region had become a prison:

> Every house a den, every man bound: the shadows are fill'd
> With spectres, and the windows wove over with curses of iron:
> Over the doors "Thou shalt not," & over the chimneys "Fear" is written:
> With bands of iron round their necks fasten'd into the walls
> The citizens, in leaden gyves the inhabitants of suburbs
> Walk heavy; soft and bent are the bones of the villagers.
> (243)

Those in power are ruthless in enforcing their rule. When threatened by the 'thought-creating fires' of revolutionary Orc, the Kings in *The Song of Los* (1795) call for famine and disease to bow the necks of the people:

> "Shall not the King call for Famine from the heath,
> "Nor the Priest for Pestilence from the fen,
> "To restrain, to dismay, to thin
> "The inhabitants of mountain and plain,
> "In the day of full-feeding prosperity
> "And the night of delicious songs?

> "Shall not the Councillor throw his curb
> "Of Poverty on the laborious,
> "To fix the price of labour,
> "To invent allegoric riches?
>
> "And the privy admonishers of men
> "Call for fires in the City,
> "For heaps of smoking ruins
> "In the night of prosperity & wantonness?
>
> "To turn man from his path,
> "To restrain the child from the womb,
> "To cut off the bread from the city,
> "That the remnant may learn to obey... (247)

Free Society

Despite his devastating critique of his contemporary world, Blake did not despair. He offered an alternative system of values and believed that it was possible to create a new society which would be both free and fulfilling. The first thing to do was to get rid of repressive religion, loveless marriage and war. As 'An ancient Proverb' has it:

> Remove away that black'ning church:
> Remove away that marriage hearse:
> Remove away that man of blood:
> You'll quite remove the ancient curse. (176)

Blake does not elaborate a comprehensive and rigid moral code. Like the Brethren of the Free Spirit, he goes beyond conventional definitions of good and evil to suggest Divine Humanity is incapable of sin.[28] As an antinomian and anarchist, he admires Jesus precisely because he rejected moral principles and broke the ten commandments. Nevertheless, Blake's fundamental values do come through in his writing. They are both simple and sublime, available to every person regardless of wealth or rank or intelligence.

Jesus personified what Blake valued most: forgiveness, energy, and creativity. Blake shaped Jesus in his mythology to his own subversive and revolutionary ends and argued that he rejected all hierarchies and tyrannies: 'The Kingdom of Heaven is the direct Negation of Earthly domination' (407). Even the summation of Jesus's teaching in the golden rule of loving one's neighbour can be applied too rigidly: 'He has observ'd the Golden Rule', Blake writes, 'Till he's become the Golden Fool' (540). The key to Christianity for Blake is not to be found in the threat of punishment but in forgiveness: 'The Gospel is Forgiveness of Sins & has No Moral Precepts' (395).

Blake is totally opposed to a stoical or repressive approach to life; in a marginal note to Lavater, he observes that 'True Christian philosophy' teaches the 'most refined Epicurism' and the maximum amount of enjoyment (75). And while accepting the claims of both sensual and intellectual pleasure, Blake believes that the highest degree of enjoyment comes from creative energy: 'Energy is Eternal Delight' (149). He knew of no other Christianity and no other Gospel than the 'liberty both of body & mind to exercise the Divine Arts of Imagination' (716-17).

Just as Blake refused to develop a rigid moral code, so he declined to elaborate a formal blue print of a free society. He does however suggest what direction a free society might take. Early in his life, the experience of the American and French Revolutions had filled him with hope. In the Songs of Innocence (1789) he sketched a picture of how things might be: caring elders look after children playing on the echoing green; chimney sweepers leap and laugh in the sun; black and white children respect and love each other; and thousands of little boys and girls sing together in the presence of wise guardians. All is infant joy. The 'Divine Image', Blake was convinced, could shine through humanity.

> For Mercy has a human heart,
> Pity a human face,
> And Love, the human form divine,
> And Peace, the human dress.

> Then every man, of every clime,
> That prays in his distress,
> Prays to the human form divine,
> Love, Mercy, Pity, Peace.   (117)

Two years later, Blake in *The French Revolution* (1791) looked forward to the imminent realization of heaven on earth:

> "Then the valleys of France shall cry to the soldier:
>   'Throw down thy sword and musket,
> " 'And run and embrace the meek peasant'. Her Nobles
>   shall hear and shall weep, and put off
> "The red robe of terror, the crown of oppression, the
>   shoes of contempt, and unbuckle
> "The girdle of war from the desolate earth; then the
>   Priest in his thund'rous cloud
> "Shall weep, bending to earth, embracing the valleys, and
>   putting his hand to the plow,
> "Shall say: 'No more I curse thee; but now I will bless
>   thee...'   (144)

Even as the Revolution in France was degenerating into the Terror, Blake could end *The Marriage of Heaven and Hell* (1790-1793) with 'A Song of Liberty' in which the fiery spirit of revolution is born. He overthrows the jealous king, and stamping the 'stony law' to dust, cries: 'EMPIRE IS NO MORE! AND NOW THE LION & WOLF SHALL CEASE' (160). The Chorus prophesizes a time of sexual and social freedom:

> Let the Priests of the Raven of dawn, no longer in deadly black, with hoarse note curse the sons of joy. Nor his accepted brethren – whom, tyrant, he calls free – lay the bound or build the roof. Nor pale religious letchery call that virginity that wishes but acts not!
>   For every thing that lives is Holy.   (160)

The crabbed and compressed Urizen, symbol of authority and tyranny, will be replaced by Albion who, rising 'from where he labour'd at the Mill with Slaves' (160) will dance in joy and freedom, naked and open-armed.

In his *Visions of the Daughters of Albion* (1793), Blake further called for a sexual and political revolution which would bring an end to the 'mistaken Demon' whose rigid patriarchal code divides mind and body and turns women and children into objects to be possessed. He yearned for love to become as 'free as the mountain wind' (194) and for the whole of creation to behold 'eternal joy' (195). In the same year, he summarized his love of freedom and his affirmation of life in a notebook:

> He who binds to himself a joy
> Does the winged life destroy;
> But he who kisses the joy as it flies
> Lives in eternity's sun rise.   (179)

Unfortunately historical developments were to prove that Blake's confidence in imminent revolution was ill founded. When Britain declared war on revolutionary France, the party of Church and State triumphed. By the turn of the century, Blake and Godwin both fell with liberty into one common grave. His *Songs of Experience* (1789-1794) showed graphically how terrible things had become. But while he came to see life more tragically, he still lived in the hope of rebuilding Jerusalem and ending the divisions in humanity and society. He held firm to the Divine Image in times of darkness and strife. Born in an age of revolutions, he never lost his confidence that out of the dialectic of innocence and experience, liberty and authority, reason and imagination, a higher synthesis of the whole person in a free society would emerge.

With Pitt's 'Gagging Acts' soon introduced after the outbreak of war with France, and Church and King mobs ready to hunt down the mildest radical, Blake realized that 'To defend the Bible in this year 1798 would cost a man his life'. It was a time, he wrote, when 'The Beast [of the State] & the Whore [of the Church] rule without control' (383). But he did not silence himself. Instead he chose the same path as the persecuted Ranters in the English Revolution who developed a secret language to carry on a wary and clandestine propaganda.[29] He was aware of what Paine called 'the Bastille of the word', the tyranny of language with fixed meanings, and sought to create a language of private meaning so that he could express his thoughts through his own symbols.[30] He therefore disguised his revolutionary and libertarian message in prophetic allegories to escape the censor and the hangman. To those who are ready to make the effort to find the key to his language and mythology, his message is plain enough. For all the complex symbolism and misty rhetoric of the prophetic writings, Blake's Jerusalem is not a religious fantasy or political utopia, but the vision of a free society which he believed would be realized on earth one day.

In the *Book of Urizen* (1794), Blake first developed his own creation myth of the material world and humanity, in which Urizen, the God of Reason, is the Creator. It offers the starkest account of the Fall of Man. The creation involves Los, the central figure in Blake's thought, who represents the poetic genius or imagination. From Los emerges his Emanation, Enitharmon, his female counterpart. But the world does not remain under the eternal rule of the tyrant Urizen who tries to entangle humanity in the net of religion, for the offspring of Los and Enitharmon is Orc, the spirit of revolt. In *The Book of Los* (1795), the myth is continued with Los creating the sun and forcing Urizen to create the material world, thereby compelling him to define and act so that he can be overcome. In *The Book of Ahania* (1795), Urizen casts out his Emanation, or Pleasure. The theme continues in *Europe: A Prophecy* (1794) with the coming of war between England and France, heralded by Enitharmon imposing her dominion on the world. But terrible Orc is still ready waiting for the coming revolution: 'And in the vineyards of red France appear'd the light of his fury' (245).

Although Blake began to express himself increasingly in the convoluted allegories of his prophetic writings, his libertarian vision shone as brightly as before. In swelling rhetoric, he may have presented the revolution in the apocalyptic language of the Gnostic sects, in terms of a Last Judgement bringing about the Everlasting Gospel in Jerusalem, but the celebration of moral, sexual and social freedom is as vigorous and enthusiastic as ever. *Vala, or the Four Zoas*, written between 1795 and 1804, is full of prophetic gloom, but at the end Los and Enitharmon build Jerusalem. With the sound of the trumpet of the Last Judgement:

> The thrones of Kings are shaken, they have lost their
>   robes & crowns,
> The poor smite their oppressors, they awake up to the
>   harvest,
> The naked warriors rush together down to the sea shore
> Trembling before the multitudes of slaves now set at
>   liberty:
> They are become like wintry flocks, like forests strip'd of
>   leaves:
> The oppressed pursue like the wind; there is no room for
>   escape.[31]   (357)

Out of the inevitable struggle of heaven and hell, innocence and experience, intellectual and physical war, Blake was convinced that Jerusalem, the city within and without, could be built. In his preface to *Milton*, written between 1804-1808, when radical political hopes were at a nadir in Britain, Blake exclaims:

> Rouze up, O Young Men of the New Age! set your foreheads against the ignorant Hirelings! For we have Hirelings in the Camp, the Court & the University, who would, if they could, for ever depress Mental & prolong Corporeal War.   (480)

He recommits himself to the intellectual and social struggle:

> I will not cease from Mental Fight,
> Nor shall my Sword sleep in my hand
> Till we have built Jerusalem
> In England's green & pleasant Land.   (481)

Milton foretells that the Children of Jerusalem will be saved from slavery. They will be redeemed from the tyrannic law of 'Satan, the Selfhood', the creator of natural religion and the legislator of moral laws which curb the passions. But in order for the 'Eternal Man' to be free, it will first be necessary to destroy the 'Negation of the Reasoning Power' in man by self-examination. In Blake's dialectic, it is necessary to negate the negation. Milton, the inspired man, declares:

> "There is a Negation, & there is a Contrary:
> "The Negation must be destroy'd to redeem the
>   Contraries.
> "The Negation is the Spectre, the Reasoning Power in
>   Man:
> "This is a false Body, an Incrustation over my Immortal
> "Spirit, a Selfhood which must be put off & annihilated
>   alway.
> "To cleanse the Face of my Spirit by Self-examination,
>
> "To bathe in the Waters of Life, to wash off the Not
>   Human,
> "I come to Self-annihilation & the grandeur of
>   Inspiration,
> "To cast off Rational Demonstration by Faith in the
>   Saviour,
> "To cast off the rotten rags of Memory by Inspiration,
> "To cast off Bacon, Locke & Newton from Albion's
>   covering,
> "To take off his filthy garments & clothe him with
>   Imagination,
> "To cast aside from Poetry all that is not Inspiration,
> "That it no longer shall dare to mock with the aspersions
>   of Madness
> "Cast on the Inspired by the tame high finisher of paltry
>   Blots
> "Indefinite, or paltry Rhymes, or paltry Harmonies,
> "Who creeps into State Government like a caterpiller to
>   destroy...   (533)

In Blake's great culminating statement *Jerusalem*, completed in 1820, the oppression of Church and State is at last cast off. Humanity realizes its divine potential and lives in peace and love. The moral law, imposed as a curse, is no longer valid. The division between the sexes ceases and the Eternal Man bearing the stamp of the Divine Image stalks the land from Amazonia to Siberia. Within every person, Blake insists, there is Jerusalem:

> In Great Eternity every particular Form gives forth or
> Emanates
> Its own peculiar Light, & the Form is the Divine Vision
> And the Light is his Garment. This is Jerusalem in every
> Man,
> A Tent & Tabernacle of Mutual Forgiveness, Male &
> Female Clothings.
> And Jerusalem is called Liberty among the Children of
> Albion. (684)

In his old age, Blake's revolutionary views inevitably made him an outsider. A republican and an anarchist, he could hardly feel at home in Tory England. Apart from Godwin and Hazlitt, nearly all the old radicals of his generation had died or lost their way. In 1827, he wrote to a friend, 'since the French Revolution Englishmen are all Intermeasurable One by Another, Certainly a happy state of Agreement to which I for One do not Agree' (878). In the same year, in his annotations to Thornton's *New Translation of the Lord's Prayer*, Blake offered his own liturgy. It shows that for all the complexity of his imaginative world and the depth of his alienation from the everyday world, he was still calling for economic justice and social freedom to prevail on earth. He continued to pray for an end to capitalist exploitation (Price), repressive morality (Satan), and political authority (Caesar). Praying to Jesus, not God, he declares:

> Give us This Eternal Day our own right Bread by taking away Money or debtor Tax & Value or Price, as we have all Things Common among us. Every thing has as much right to Eternal Life as God, who is the Servant of Man. His Judgment shall be Forgiveness that he may be consum'd in his own Shame.
> Leave us not in Parsimony, Satan's Kingdom; liberate us from the Natural man & [*words illegible*] Kingdom.
> For thine is the Kingdom & the Power & the Glory & not Caesar's or Satan's. Amen. (788)

V. Nebuchadnezzar, symbol of reason, authority and oppression, being banished from Jerusalem
(By pemission of The Tate Gallery, London)

Blake's prophetic vision is not merely that of a spiritual New Age. His view of paradise has its roots in the 'sunny side' of eighteenth-century London life as well as in the hills, sky and sea of the Sussex coast.[32] He is undoubtedly a visionary, but he combines mysticism with social radicalism and common sense. He valued above all bread, music and the laughter of children. He asked for a fair price for the depiction of ideal beauty. Like the Brethren of the Free Spirit and the Ranters before him, like Godwin in his own day, and Kropotkin later, his vision is of a free society which transcends conventional politics and the struggle for power and which ensures that every individual is 'King & Priest in his own House' (879). It is a society based on mutual aid, for 'Brotherhood is Religion' (689); and complete forbearance, for 'What is Liberty without Universal Toleration?' (413). It is a society which would allow communal individuality to flourish, combining voluntary cooperation with personal autonomy. Men and women would live in sexual equality and enjoy free love. Human relations would no longer be corroded by the cash nexus. Workers would receive the product of their labour and all would enjoy the fruits of the earth in common. Human beings would be able to realize their creative natures and be free to exercise the 'Divine Arts of Imagination' (716-17).

While Blake dramatically pictures transformed humanity in a free society in harmony with nature, it is not a utopian dream or a mystical fantasy. 'Every thing possible to be believ'd is an image of truth' (151), he reminds us, and 'Truth can never be told so as to be understood, and not be believ'd' (152). He may have been a visionary but he was not content with passive contemplation. He interpreted the world in his own way but he also wanted to change it.

Blake made no shallow distinction between theory and practice since 'Thought is Act' (400). At the same time, he believed that one could begin to realize a free society here and now. It is not necessary to wait for a cataclysmic upheaval or divine intervention. Everyone can begin to change society by changing their own lives: 'Whenever any Individual Rejects Error & Embraces Truth, a Last Judgment passes upon that Individual' (613). If one cleanses the

VI. *'Europe supported by Africa & America'*, engraving for J.G. Stedman, *Narrative* (1796)
(*By permission of the British Library*)

doors of perception, one will see everything as it is, infinite, living and holy. Blake believed that the political is the personal, and called for individual rebellion in everyday life even while working for a total transformation of society.

In his own life, Blake was an outsider, an eccentric living in virtual internal exile. He lived in a State of 'Empire or Tax' (777) in which on his own account all visionary men were accounted madmen. Yet we can now see him at the centre of the Age of Revolution in which he lived and as a key figure in English Romanticism.

We continue to live in a very similar world, with warring Nation States threatening to engulf the whole world in an unimaginable cataclysm. Instrumental reason, unchecked by feeling and uninformed by the imagination, coolly plans the total annihilation of humanity and the complete destruction of the earth. The machine still dominates human beings who are divided within, from each other, and from nature. The agents of Urizen are still at large.

For this reason, Blake's message remains as potent and relevant as ever. He offers the prophetic vision of a free community of fully realized individuals who act from impulse and who are artists, kings and priests in their own right. Neglected in his own day, distorted by posterity, Blake's sun is beginning to rise as the post-industrial society approaches and the love of freedom grows stronger every day.

NOTES

1. J. Bronowski suggested 'anarchism remains masterful in Blake's prophetic books' (*William Blake and the Age of Revolution* (London: Routledge & Kegan Paul, 1972), p. 68) but referred to it not so much as a coherent social philosophy but as a form of visceral revolt. While G. R. Sabri-Tabrizi insists in *The 'Heaven' and 'Hell' of William Blake* (London: Lawrence & Wishart, 1973) that Blake is a historical materialist, the Marxist critic Edward Larrissy stresses the 'libertarian' nature of Blake's work (*William Blake* (Oxford: Blackwell, 1985), p.111). After concluding that Blake was an anarchist in rejecting all forms of imposed authority, I came across Peter Cadogan's assertion that 'the real founder of English anarchism was and remains William Blake' in the *Bulletin of Anarchist Research* 11 (August 1987), p. 3.

2. For Blake's alleged change of heart, see Kathleen Raine, *William Blake* (London: Thames & Hudson, 1970), p. 52.

3. Algernon Charles Swinburne, *William Blake: A Critical Essay* (London: Chatto & Windus, 1906), p. 332. For Blake as a 'Liberty Boy' see Alexander Gilchrist, *The Life of William Blake*, 2 vols. (London, 1863).

4. All quotations are taken from *Blake: Complete Writings*, edited by Geoffrey Keynes (Oxford University Press, 1972). The number given in brackets after each quotation in the text refers to the page number in this edition.

5. Seymour Kirkup, quoted by Mona Wilson in *The Life of William Blake*, edited by Geoffrey Keynes (Oxford University Press, 1971), p. 267.

6. Alexander Gilchrist, quoted by Wilson, ibid., p. 81.

7. Bronowski, *William Blake*, op. cit., p. 112.

8. Samuel Palmer, quoted in *William Blake: Songs of Innocence and Experience*, edited by Margaret Bottrall (London: Macmillan, 1970), p. 53.

9. Peter Kropotkin, *The State: Its Historic Role* (London: Freedom Press, 1987), p. 59.

10. For an account of the radical aspects of the Dissenting tradition, see my *William Godwin* (London and New Haven: Yale University Press, 1984), chapter iii and passim.

11. See Norman Cohn, *The Pursuit of the Millennium: Revolutionary Millenarians and Mystical Anarchists of the Middle Ages* (London: Paladin, 1984).

12. See Christopher Hill, *The World Turned Upside Down: Radical Ideas During the English Revolution* (Harmondsworth: Penguin, 1978).

13 See A. L. Morton, *The Everlasting Gospel: A Study in the Sources of William Blake* (London: Lawrence & Wishart, 1958), p. 35.

14 See E. P. Thompson, 'London', *Interpreting Blake*, edited by Michael Phillips (Cambridge University Press, 1978), pp. 13-14.

15 T. S. Eliot, 'Blake', *William Blake: Songs of Innocence and Experience*, op. cit., pp. 96-97.

16 See Mary Raine, *Blake and Tradition* (London: Routledge & Kegan Paul, 1969), I, p.ll.

17 Mary Wollstonecraft, *Mary and The Wrongs of Women*, edited by Gary Kelly (Oxford University Press, 1976), p. 68.

18 See Larrissy, *William Blake*, op. cit., p. 123.

19 See Wilson, *The Life of William Blake*, op. cit., p. 66.

20 See David N. Erdman, *Blake: Prophet against Empire: A Poet's Interpretation of the History of his Own Times* (Princeton, New Jersey: Princeton University Press, 1977), pp. 113-14.

21 For the ironic meaning of this work, see Morton D. Paley, *Energy and the Imagination: A Study of the Development of Blake's Thought* (Oxford: Clarendon Press, 1970), p. 171; and Erdman, Blake, op. cit., p. 449.

22 See Morton, *The Everlasting Gospel*, op. cit., p. iii.

23 See Cohn, *The Pursuit of the Millennium*, op. cit., pp. 173, 178.

24 See Wilson, *The Life of William Blake*, op. cit., p. 72.

25 Raine, *Blake and Tradition*, op. cit., I, p. 212.

26 Edmund Burke, *Reflections on the Revolution in France*, edited by Conor Cruise O'Brien (Harmondsworth: Penguin, 1969), p. 170.

27 See Thompson, 'London', *Interpreting Blake*, op. cit., pp. 200-201.

28 See Cohn, *The Pursuit of the Millennium*, op. cit., p. 173.

29 Ibid., p. 296.

30 See Olivia Smith, *The Politics of Language 1791-1819* (Oxford: Clarendon Press, 1984), p. 139.

31 For the political nature of this poem, see my review of the French translation by J. Blondel, Oeuvres, IV (Paris: Aubier Flammarion, 1983), in *Etudes Anglaises* XXXVIII, 2 (1985), pp. 235-236.

32 Erdman, Blake, op. cit., p. 3.